Open Collar:

How to Work From Home in 9 Easy Steps

By

Kimberley Suter

Why you should buy this book.

With the economy downslide over the past few years, more and more people are without "real" jobs. You had no choice but to work from home. The real go-getters have been really successful at their home office.

If you've been thinking about leaving the rat race of the city office, or have been forced to leave, now is your chance to make it on your own on your own terms.

The question is how? You need a plan.

This book will take you by the hand to guide you through the basics of setting up your home office space, setting schedules and more. You may already have an idea of what you want to work at, you may have been working for someone else using all of your knowledge. Now you want to (or have to) do it on your own. This book will guide you though the beginning steps of working from home with your "open collar".

We've all heard of the Blue collar worker, and the White collar worker. There's a new one in town. The **"Open Collar"** worker is the worker who works from home. The whole term "open collar worker" suggests many things. Open to new ideas. Relaxed atmosphere. Working at your own pace.

For Dan,

You really should start your new career at home.

Introduction

We've all heard of the Blue collar worker, and the White collar worker. There's a new one in town. The "Open Collar" worker is the worker who works from home. The whole term "open collar worker" suggests many things. Open to new ideas. Relaxed atmosphere. Working at your own pace.

Home-based entrepreneurship has been growing in numbers. "Open-collar workers" come from many backgrounds: downsized workers, stay-at-home parents, disabled people, entertainers, writers, inventors and more.

The main intention is to work on their own schedules, devote time to what they love and be their own bosses.

This book is for those who have a plan, want a home office, those people already working at home, and those who are still deciding whether to start a home business.

Working from home sounds like the dream job. Wake up whenever you want to, shower around noon, spend the whole day drinking coffee, checking emails and snacking on delicious cookies. Let's find out what it really takes to work from home.

Let's start with how much money you'll save by working at home.

Chapter 1 - 10 Ways to Save Money by Working at Home

In an era awash with technology and a new independent spirit it is becoming increasingly more feasible for people to start working from home. While this can be very scary and seem like a huge leap for some people it can be helpful to consider how working from home can save a huge amount of money.

1. Commute Savings

The difference between commuting and not commuting is a lot of money in your pocket. When someone starts working from home they no longer have to pay for that gas it requires to commute. It means that someone doesn't have to buy a train pass, or bus tickets. This is all a bunch of money that working from home saves you. It could be literally thousands of dollars of savings!

2. Food

Eating out is expensive, and people who work in an office are much more likely to go to restaurants or office cafeterias for lunch. Buying food in bulk and from grocery stores is dramatically cheaper than going to a cafeteria or restaurant every day. Working from home saves a ton of money on food costs.

3. Coffee

Okay, so who isn't a little addicted to Starbucks coffee? Though, at about $5 a cup this is one addiction that hurts the wallets of those who suffer from it. Working from home makes it easier to have coffee at home, where, for the same quality, you can save a lot of money. Working from home saves you money that you might be wasting at Starbucks. At least $5 per day 5 days a week, 50ish weeks a year? That's over $1000!

4. Clothes

When you work at an office you spend an exorbitant amount of money on clothing costs. This involves buying expensive shirts and suits which cost a ton of money, to maintain what many offices consider a "professional wardrobe". When you work at home unless you are Skyping into meetings, you can dress comfortable casual -- what you would normally wear at home. Might as well be comfortable, you are at home after all!

5. Tax Breaks

Working from home can also help supply you with many tax breaks. These tax breaks include numerous deductions from office space, property taxes, maintenance, and business expenses. These tax breaks add up. You can claim all of these as expenses every year. You can also charge yourself rent.

6. Less Time and Higher Salary

Commuting an hour to and from work every day is no small period of time. This time is saved when you don't have to commute. This raises "real" income of those who work from home because more time is spent working and less time is spent trying to get to work. This free time really adds up remarkably quickly and contributes to even more saved money.

7. Less Stress

Those who work from home experience markedly less stress than those who go into an office for work every weekday. This means that those who work from home have much less stress during the day. Stress and good health have a direct and undeniable correlation and with good health comes lower medical bills and more money in your pocket.

8. Car Maintenance

The cost of not driving a car miles every day makes it far less likely that a car will need to be serviced. Less car maintenance means more money saved.

9. Child Care

Those with children know that working from an office means paying for daycare. Daycare is expensive. Although working from home won't necessarily mean no childcare, it will mean less childcare is necessary and that will save tons of money. If your children are in school, you'll be able to drop them off and pick them up or be there when they get off the bus, just like a stay-at-home parent.

10. Dry Cleaning

Nice clothes require frequent and professional dry cleaning and working from home negates this expen$e entirely.

Now that you know all the benefits of saving money by working at home, let's make sure you keep that money in your pocket by avoiding work at home scams.

Chapter 2 - Avoiding Work from Home Scams

The internet is now part of our everyday lives. It offers a global marketplace for *e-business*. But there are no responsible gatekeepers on the "information superhighway." This new, unregulated technology means great opportunities for consumers, investors, businesses — and for crooks.

The rapid rise of Internet use brings misleading promotions, bogus travel offers, lotteries, contests and other illegal practices. It's sometimes very hard to tell the difference between criminals who use the Internet to rob people and reputable online businesses.

You can protect yourself by learning to recognize the signs of "Work At Home" Schemes. However, if you have ever been a victim of this fraud, it's important to report the scam quickly so that law enforcement agencies can shut the fraudulent operations down.

The simple definition of **work-at-home scam** is a get-rich-quick scheme in which a person is lured by an offer to be employed at home usually through an advertisement and often they are required to perform some simple task within a specified timeline with a large amount of income that far exceeds the market rate for the type of work.

The main purpose of such an offer is to extort money from the person, either by making the person invest in their products whose resale value is usually misrepresented or charging a fee to sign up to the scheme.

Work-at-home opportunities are no way to make money. The flashy banner advertisements typically promise a "six figure income" for working on projects "in great demand."
Here are the telltale signs of work-at-home scams:

- They use personal testimonials but they hide the true identity of who made them.

- They assure you of guaranteed markets and a demand for your hard work.

- They request for a fee for instructions before even letting you know how the plan works.

- They tell you that no experience is required.

- They never offer you regular salaried employment.

- They promise you huge profits and big part-time earnings.

- Don't judge a web site by how it looks.

How to Avoid Work-at-Home Scams

- Always remember that most people in cyberspace are not always what they seem.

- Research on the company's track record before making any decisions.

- Understand what's being offered at the table, its merits and demerits.

- Never respond to bulk e-mails. It's best to keep your distance if they do not know you.

- Beware of investing your hard earned money in an opportunity you learn about over the Internet.

- Make sure the company has a legit phone number and a physical address and not just an e-mail address or post office box.

- Be cautious about giving out your personal or financial information.

- Use common sense. If you have a gut feeling that something is not right, then it isn't.

- Don't take other users' ID's for granted. Online user profiles and personal information provided by others could be more fiction than fact.

- When first joining a chat room or news group, read along for a while before joining the conversation to get a feel for the discussion and participants. If the newsgroup or chat room has a charter or FAQ "Frequently Asked Questions" read it before signing up.

- Protect your password. People can use your online password to log on to your email account, send mail from it or otherwise run up expenses. Use a combination of letters, numbers for your password, change it and do not share it with anyone.

- Emails are always private. Most are read by the sender and recipient only, but sometimes others may have access to it. Also, one incorrect letter in an e-mail address can send the message to the wrong recipient. Your message can be forwarded to others inadvertently. Unless you're encrypting your e-mail, it's no more private than a postcard.

- Be Careful when providing credit card information. Use of secure servers is automatic in major Web browsers, and most Web sites that support them will clearly mark that option. Make sure you get a message that a secure server is in use before sending information.

- Be careful with downloads. When downloading software to listen to music, play games or browse pictures, there is a potential threat that you may be exposing your computer to, including downloading Viruses, Trojans and Malwares that will damage your computer files or sends out your personal information anonymously to the scam artists. A suitable solution would be to download software from a trusted vendor and conduct regular scans on the files using virus detection software.

- Do not enter contests operated by unfamiliar companies. Fraudulent scam artists and online marketers every now and then use contest entry forms to identify potential victims and get their personal information.

- Identify how the company handles their complaints. It a tedious task to resolve complaints, especially if two parties come from different countries. Look for credible reviews and information about the company standards on different websites for reliability and how they have managed to handle disputes.

To conclude, most work-at-home scams — envelope stuffing — all you get for your money are step by step instructions to place an advertisement like the one that led you to sign up with them. Once recruited, the only way you can make any money is to recruit other would-be workers.

A new trend in the recent schemes is that they do not actually offer work at home jobs, but sell ideas for setting up profitable home businesses. This involves selling you materials and products for making low-demand items that you will have to sell.

WORK-AT-HOME SCAMS ARE MEANT TO TAKE YOUR MONEY BUT NEVER RETURN THE PROMISED **"EMPLOYMENT OPPORTUNITIES."**

Avoid them at all cost. They'll rip you off.

Now that you know how to protect yourself at home while working, what are you going to work at? Are you passionate about your hobby or have you been dreaming about being your own boss. Read on for help on pursuing your dream.

Chapter 3 - Follow your Passion and follow your Dream - What you are good at?

Most of us don't get opportunities to follow our passion by the mere stroke of luck. There are many who failed to pursue their dreams in life or to tread along the path at which they were really good. Regret is a terrible thing, and a dream is powerful enough to bring you regret if you don't take the chance to at least follow it. Your dreams have no limits, you are the creator of your dreams, big or small. When this is understood, you are able to design a way to favour you plan and accomplish your end goal.

Perhaps you've "always wanted to..." This is a passion. This is a dream. This is a goal. When you start to pursue your dream, you will face challenges you never could have foretold. But nothing will stop you. You will surprise yourself at your ability to work through any situation. You will feel excited and energized by the life you are choosing to live. You will be so excited to go to work every morning. Or should I say stay home to work. You will feel proud of what you are doing. And you will like yourself more for it.

"Peter" was a brilliant student and as far as his academic records go Peter never stood second in university. But, Peter failed to pursue his dream of becoming an entrepreneur. The example of many a "Peter" is well represented in the words of Bill Gates. Bill Gates once said that he never stood first in any university; but hired many. On the contrary had "Peter" been able to follow his passion and dream, the world may have got another Bill Gates or Steve Jobs.

Hopefully you can identify your true passion and dream early in life so that you can follow the same whole heartedly with passion and dedication for making a difference in life. Mind that a dream is not what you see when your eyes are closed; rather it is what you see when your eyes are open. Even if you are starting a new career in a new field it's not too late. NOW is the time to make your dreams come true.

If you haven't decided yet what your new at home career will be, you have a lot of options. Almost all real opportunities won't require you to part with any money to get started, and the Internet is your friend when it comes to research.

Just a few opportunities that you might want to consider include web design, freelance writing, virtual administration, blogging, writing, editing, and translation work, selling items that you make, selling your inventions. Most of these do require some expertise, of course, but if you already have the skills, it makes sense to work out ways in which you can monetize them.   If you are a writer or blogger, check out freelance job sites like: bloggingpro.com or journalismjobs.com and join www.LinkedIn.com, and check out their Jobs tab.   Also, you can do specific keyword searches on Google and Twitter to find more sites looking for writers and contributors.

For freelancers of any type, graphic designers, artists, IT, website develpment, mobile app builders, data entry, translators, transcribers --you can do just about anything. Check out elance.com, guru.com, or freelancer.com.

If you have absolutely no clue what you want to do, what is your favorite hobby?   Can you monetize it? In order to stay motivated in your home career you need to love what you do. As they say, if you love your job, you'll never work another day in your life.

Your dreams and passions will change over time, so don't think that everything is set in stone. It should be a work in progress rather than a definitive document. Looking back in 12 months, or even just 3 months down the line can be extremely rewarding when you realize just how much you've achieved.

"Love what you do and do what you love. Don't listen to anyone else who tells you not to do it. You do what you want, what you love. Imagination should be the center of your life." - Ray Bradbury

Ok, now you have an idea of what you want to work at from home. Now you need a workspace. Let's get some ideas on how to create that office.

Chapter 4 - How to Create an Organized and Distraction Free Work Space At Home

Recent statistics show that quite a number of people are starting a business and becoming their own boss and over 60% of these businesses are started from home. There's a great graphic at this website to illustrate the increase in telecommuting http://www.payscale.com/career-news/2012/03/working-from-home. Could this be an option for you?

Up and down the world, people are spotting gaps in the market and realizing there are customers for the skills, knowledge or assets they have developed through employment or personal passions. These entrepreneurs are using their home space to bring business ideas to fruition.

There are a lot of benefits to a home-based business, including the 60-second commute, being able to build a business around family life, and reduced overheads from not having to pay for commercial premises.

This is why people choose to start at home businesses. We're now seeing growing home businesses make full use of technology and communications to reach customers, generate income and profits without having to expand out of their home space.

One of the great benefits of basing the business at home is the ability to work where and how you like, while wearing what you like! Here, we will look at ways to create an environment that will suit and equip your office with the tools and accessories that will deliver a productive end result.

Find dedicated space

Try to create an area in the house that functions as your dedicated workspace. That way you can mentally adjust yourself to be in business mode when in that space. It helps you to know when you should be working and when you should be taking a break.

It will also help make it clear to friends and family that when you're in your home office or studio, you're working. And when the door's closed, it means, 'I'm busy. Please don't disturb'.

A light touch -- Lots of light is good for your mood and work pace but avoid too much task-light shining on the computer monitor. As for colours on the walls, go for light shades as they will make the space look bigger, and consider mirrors to bounce light around.

This dedicated space could be a spare room, in the attic, under the stairs or even the garden shed.

A Spring Clean

Depending on the nature of your business, you could be wondering what to do with all the stuff in the room that you want to use as your home office? Invest in storage boxes and turn your closets into filing cabinets! Or buy big boxes, label them well and then find a place to hide them away; maybe doubling up as a chair for visitors. Got extra stuff from that room that you are never going to use? Box them up and send to a recycling company, or second hand store or have a yard sale. Clear the clutter.

Invest in a good desk and chair

Spend time buying an office chair. Sit in each one of the chairs on display. Make sure it's both sturdy and comfortable! It should be a chair that's designed for computer use – and try it out first at a desk in the store, to make sure you can adjust the chair's height to suit you. Ideally, your feet should be flat on the floor and your back straight. Getting this right will make working from home so much more comfortable!

Get a good, sturdy desk. Measure your space first, make sure the desk is the right size for the room. If the desk is too big, you will feel crowded and not comfortable. Get a cheaper beginner desk if you have to, to start and get your dream desk later when the money starts rolling in.

Vision board

Set goals and stay on track with the use of a vision board. A vision board is a visual reminder of what you're trying to achieve in your business and personal life and, attached to the home office wall, can act as a useful daily prompt and pep talk. More on goals later!

Buy a basic board and stick to it pictures that represent your ambitions; places you want to visit, targets for the company, and people with whom you enjoy spending time. You will be able to glance at it each day to remind yourself of everything you're working for and towards and to measure how the business is doing. Such a board will encourage you to stay motivated and hit the targets you've set as well as maintaining the bigger picture of where you want the business to go. If you've heard of the book "The Secret" this is what it is all about.   Visualizing your goal and making it happen.

The top of your vision board is a visual reminder of what you're trying for as a high level goal achievement in your business and personal life.

Try a virtual vision board with www.pinterest.com and bookmark it.

Tech fit-out

A computer, monitor, keyboard and mouse. When it comes to equipping your home office with IT, this needn't mean starting from scratch or spending lots of money. Once your business grows you can upgrade your technology as and when funds become available. To start with, there are affordable solutions that can get you up and running in no time at all – you may have some of them already!

Computer

When starting out, using your home's shared computer or personal laptop will be just fine. Bear in mind, however, that in the first few months of starting your business you may find yourself working more hours than usual, trying to get it all set up – so prepare cohabiting friends and family for the possibility of reduced access!

Also, when your business grows, the data you accumulate – information on your customers, clients and contacts, including financial details – will become more and more valuable. You might then think twice about sharing your computer with the rest of the family.

For that reason, and the flexibility you'll have in deciding when and where you can work, you might consider buying a separate laptop computer. There was a time when doing so was much more expensive than buying a desktop computer, but in recent years the prices have almost leveled off.

The Monitor

The monitor or monitors (you can have more than one these days) should be at eye level and the monitor itself about an arm's length away from you. Set the monitor's brightness so that it isn't fatiguing for the eyes.

Multifunction printer

Imagine keeping a printer, scanner, photocopier and fax machine in one home office – you'd have no room to do any work! This is where multifunction printers come in as they enable you to have full functionality in one device and act as real space-savers!   The printers are actually quite inexpensive, watch for sales. It's the ink or toner that are expensive. So when you are shopping for a multifunction printer, also check the prices on the ink.

External hard drive

These are great for extending the storage capacity of your computer – so you can keep more data and programs – but they're especially useful for backing up the entirety of your machine. They're easy to set up – just plug them in and they show up in your operating system as another drive. You can then just drag and drop important folders or use special software that automates the process for you. Also when you are buying a new computer you don't need to invest big money in a machine with terabytes of memory. You can get that in a great external hard drive for a lot less money.

VoIP phones

You can make serious savings on your phone bill by using a VoIP phone. VoIP stands for voice over internet protocol and it basically means making calls over the internet rather than by using your phone line. As such, it's a much cheaper way of making calls (it's sometimes free). And it's the easiest way to set up a second phone line.

If you use VoIP or internet calling you can assign a landline-sounding phone number to your account, so you can receive calls to your desktop or laptop using a VoIP phone or divert calls to your phone when you're out and about running your other errands.

Webcam

A webcam enables you to video chat with clients and contacts and is useful when you need to have a 'face-to-face' meeting but can't get away. After all you'll be saving money by having meeting via Skype, Google Hangouts or Facetime from your home office. (You might want to get out of your pajamas on those days.)

Getting connected

You'll need broadband right from the start: during your research, while you're setting up your business, through to when it grows and takes over the world! Your two main options are ADSL broadband and cable broadband with the biggest difference being that ADSL requires a phone line, while cable broadband does not.

The advantage of cable broadband is that if you don't have a landline phone, and always use your mobile, you can save money by not having to pay line rental on your phone as well as on your internet connection. It's often faster, too, but you'll need to check whether it's available in your area. ADSL broadband is more commonplace and there are lots of companies offering it.

As always, read the fine print before you sign anything. Here are some things to look out for:

- Price – some broadband prices seem really cheap but often the prices advertised are for the first few months of an 18-month contract, so make sure you know what you're getting into before you sign anything.

- Usage – some broadband companies will set restrictions on the amount of data you can download in a month and sometimes even charge you extra if you go over your agreed limit. These limits rarely affect most users, but if your business is the kind that needs to send and receive lots of information, look for deals with generous monthly download allowances. Or, better still, unlimited bandwidth.

- Customer support – if you're installing broadband for the first time, you might need some help setting up and also, once you're up and running, knowing what to do when your connection suddenly drops. For these sorts of queries it's handy to have good customer support, so check to see what's on offer and, crucially, how much it would cost to call for help. Business stores often have young IT guys that will travel to your home office and set everything up for you for a nominal charge.

Superfast broadband

Network providers are investing billions to deliver superfast fibre broadband. If you live in an area with an activated exchange, new speeds will power your business and enable you to work faster online and download rich digital media in no time.

Network

Be connected all around the house – and even in the garden – by setting up a wireless network. Your internet service provider may have already provided you with a router – a device that allows you to share your internet connection with other computers in your home.

There are two types of wireless router: one for ADSL and another for cable internet. Check with your internet service provider to find out which is the best router for your type of connection. If you need to get a "wireless extender" it just plugs into a regular power outlet and provides a longer range for your wifi.

Other Features That Will Make the Perfect Work Space.

Great lighting

This can make a huge difference on your eyes. It's a major problem for your eyes to stare at a flickering light like a computer screen for hours on end. Ensuring that you have proper lighting will take some of the strain off of your eyes.

An Aesthetic view

It's advisable to place the desk near a window to add some natural lighting and something interesting to look at every now and again. An aesthetic pleasing view can go a long way to keeping your working sessions less boring especially if you're working out of your closet, odds are you don't have very good natural sunlight.

Good drinks: coffee, tea, etc.

A comforting beverage is great for a helpful work environment. It's a small perk, but every little bit helps.

Non-distracting music

A little jazz, world, rhythm or classical background music helps lighten the mood, and can even help focus. Some people can focus with any kind of music, but music without words typically works the best.

Short Breaks

Working with rests is incredibly critical to ensuring that you're going to get the most out of your day. These breaks improve efficiency and creativity.

Regular Exercise

This is not an option: it's a must for any homeworker or modern office. This is due to the pretty sedentary lifestyle that they have. Health can drastically go downhill if you don't take care of yourselves and exercise on a regular basis. Aside from all the health benefits of exercise, there are lots of great work benefits as well. A clear mind!

Foliage

Add some carbon-munching plants around your home office. They can provide some fun and colour to your workplace. And provide clean fresh air!

Avoid clutter

Clutter is an aesthetic problem as well as a mental problem. If your work space is cluttered it creates jumbled thinking habits. The brain needs a clean and clear surrounding and not a messy, unorganized environment. This also includes your desktop clutter as well keeping your folders and documents well organized is a great habit.

Awesome desktop wallpaper

While it's a small aesthetic thing, it can make a huge difference. Clean, fun or just different desktop patterns changed every now and again can add little spice to your workday, and can provide a slight boost.

There's no getting around it. Working environments are one of the biggest factors that affect how productive we can be throughout the day. There's a major difference between spending time in a tidy, aesthetic area or a bowling alley dumpster. Taking the time to set up suitable workspaces for your project means that you'll have an optimal workspace no matter what you're working on.

You've got a great business idea, know how to avoid some scams, let's make sure this workspace works as a great home office.

Chapter 5 - Top 10 Tips for Designing a Home Office

Home may be where the heart is, but for the brain, nowhere beats the office.

For internet business owners, an office is more just a room with a computer. It's a factory, built for the creation of ideas. The home office will serve as a boardroom, canteen, meeting room, telephone room, and more, so making it a place that feels comfortable and inspiring is a huge must.

Numerous challenges stand in the way of a person and their online success. Technology moves rapidly. Competition for income grows stronger each year. Even rival entrepreneurs constantly look to steal customers out from underneath people's noses any chance they can get. There is no rest. Your office is a vantage point. It's the position from which you execute your escape from the rat race, with the hope of reaching the promised land of financial freedom.

So how do you get the perfect home office?

Nobody has the faintest idea. They don't know, because a perfect home office doesn't exist. You probably joined this industry because of the freedoms it gives you, right? Well designing your home office makes full use of those freedoms.

While grey painted walls and inspirational kitty posters are optional, some things aren't: productivity. Your home office must help you stay efficient and profitable.

Because of that, here is a Top 10 list of tips (not rules) to help you get the most out of your place of work.

10 Create a dedicated work area

While lying in bed and working is a dream for many, it's not the best way to prepare yourself for the bigger demands that lie in wait. An 'official' area with all of your tools handy is the best way to maintain productivity, and avoid wasting time searching for pens, your cell phone, or printing paper. It's also one of the best ways to stay motivated. Treat what you do as an actual job, rather than a hobby. This will give you far greater focus, and much more drive to succeed.

9 Keep a clock on the wall

Just because there's no longer an 8am train to catch, doesn't mean punctuality stops. A regular clock will help you maintain a routine. It will also help you stay on course. A game of solitaire and a cup of coffee is great every now and again. When that game of solitaire and your beverage run over in to late afternoon, you have a problem.

8 Get a proper chair

Your back has been a loyal servant to you, and will continue to be so unless you treat it poorly. Cheap chairs will give you a place to sit, but they won't do you any favors in the long run. Great spinal posture when working at a computer can prevent a host of serious skeletal problems later in life, and will also help prevent strain related injuries now. While you don't have to spend 4 figures on a good chair, do try to get one that's been made with posture and comfort in mind.

7 Invest in good storage

Having papers and books lying everywhere will clutter up your desk. It will also increase the odds of you losing something important. Investing in some good storage options will solve this problem completely. Filing cabinets, book shelves, folders... all are things that improve space and overall usability of your work area. An organized desk shows an organized mind. Don't let your desk become a dumping ground.

6 Make it a color you love

Whether you want your office to be calming, and full of pale greens, or vibrant, and full of orange, that's fine. You know yourself best, and you know what moods get the most out of you. Sure, the offices in top law firms may be beige, and sure, the offices in call centers may be grey, but you're working for yourself now. Creative decisions are down to you, and nobody will tell you what you can and can't have.

5 Position yourself near a window

Being able to look outside is a nice break from staring at a screen for hours. Looking off into the distance is not only a great way to prevent eye strain, but it's also great for morale. Natural light and greenery are big motivators for people. So is the smell of fresh air. I'm sure you've noticed most offices try to include plants, and many workplaces will even have roof gardens or window plants. They also use special types of bright lighting which most resembles sunlight. You can have the real thing. Work with actual greenery in sight, and sit with the window slightly open. (Weather and noise distraction permitting, of course.)

#4 Pick comforting accessories

Unless you enjoy working in a traditional office space, try to pick furniture and accessories that make your work space feel like home. Rustic desks from home design stores, rugs, bendy lamps, designer blinds; whatever makes your office feel pleasant to be in will work well.

3 Avoid distraction

It's an obvious one, but it's an important point nonetheless. Working close to loud noises, or the family area isn't the smartest idea. There will be days when the slightest thing will distract you. While it's not always possible to run your office in a quiet part of the house; at least staying as far away from the TV, and your loud-music loving teenage son's bedroom, is advised.

2 Pick the right technology

Choosing the right type of computer, phone and printer will all help you work more effectively. If possible, try to take it a step further and purchase items with the least amount of wires. All-in-one computer systems like the Apple Mac, and wireless phones and printers are a thing of regularity now. Treading over wires, finding the right cables for the right device, and knocking things over should be things of the past.

If wireless devices aren't an option, at least tidy up your cables by feeding them through an encased chord. There are many wire organizers on the market now, many of which make a big difference to the space found on a workstation.

1 Inspire yourself

Whether you work at home part time, or full time, there's just something exciting about it. There's a wealth of money on the internet ready to be tapped into, and a moment of inspiration or a spark of creativity can be all you need to skyrocket your income.

There will be days when you're more distracted, and there will be days where you're lethargic. Everybody goes through these. Having inspiration around will help minimize the bad effects of them. Remind yourself why you're doing what you're doing. Have little items around that put you in a good frame of mind. Perhaps a vision or a motivational poster on the wall, or a copy of your old report card in your drawer. Even a picture of your family can help. Some choose to go down the extreme motivational route and have a picture of the sports car they wish to buy as their computer screensaver.

Whatever motivates and inspires you, keep it around. By including it in the design of your home office, and by following these tips you'll all but ensure that it remains a happy and productive place for many years to come.

Chapter 6 - How to Avoid Pitfalls

Making money from home is now a thriving opportunity. Indeed, many people have made a lot of money from working at home. Working in office is now more fashionable to some people because they earn more money from working from home on the internet than what they earn from office work. BUT, working from home does have its own pitfalls.

Family

For someone who is living with their family, it is important that you are aware that family distraction will certainly come whenever you doing your "work from home business". It is a common thing that family members will interrupt you most times you are doing your work at home. Also, do daily chores every day *before* starting work . Also, when it is time for work, don't sit back and start watching television. Eat that breakfast and tear yourself away.

Don't Isolate Yourself

Try as much as possible to stay connected to people who are doing the same kind of work you are doing on the internet. So, whenever you have problems, you can share it with them and when there is any development concerning the work you are doing, they will notify you. You should work with the notion that nobody is a repository of knowledge. That is, nobody can know everything. So, staying connected with people that are offering the same services will do a lot in making you avoid pitfalls associated with working from home.

Don't Sit Back Waiting for Jobs

You must look for jobs, don't just fall back in your chair and expect jobs to be coming in. You have to be very hard-working and look for people that want your services. Surf the internet to see those who are in need of your services and then send them an offer that is not outrageous. Don't be shy to offer your services for any firm. With diligence and hard-work, your job search will yield great results. Give your clients cutting-edge perspective on your services. Market using social media (for work). Linked In is a great way to connect with prospective clients.

Initial Costs

Working from home requires some initial start up costs. As they say, "You have to spend money to make money." The cost of laptops, cell phones, internet, office furniture, file cabinets, and other equipment needed for remote access can be really expensive.

While there are some AWESOME advantages to working at home, like not waking as early because you don't have to fight traffic on your way to work, interruptions from chatty Bob in the next cubicle, le$$ restaurant eating, and no buzzy fluorescent lights overhead all day -- there are some negatives. Believe it or not.

Deterioration of socials skills.

Now you don't see people everyday. Your family doesn't count. After a while, having a simple business conversation could be a challenge. You might actually miss that banter with Cubicle Bob. You miss out on the camaraderie that stems from working with others. There are no coworkers to go to lunch with.

Distractions

Facebook and cat or farting goat videos are definitely fun and funny, but you might think that you've only spent a few minutes, after all that video was only 1 minute and 37 seconds. It's the other linking 10 videos after it. Suddenly you're down 2 hours! Come on Farmville, give us a break! Are posts from pseudo friends really more important than making money?

The Decline of Household Duties

You may start to think that work is more important than that load of laundry or the dust on the furniture. Home can be distracting: pets will whine to be let out, children will be asking for snacks and play time, your DVR will be full of your favorite TV shows, and laundry is there waiting to be washed. It's nearly impossible not to do household chores, and spend some time watching TV or playing games. You have to make time for both fun home stuff and work. Schedule the fun if you have to. Set a time for lunch where you watch your favorite television show and throw some laundry in the wash. Explain the nature of your work to family and seek their co-operation. Delegate some of those chores you don't have time to do. Little Johnny can throw some dirty clothes in the wash. It's really only a couple of buttons to push. And he'll feel important because he's helping. Win-win!

Spouse Takes Second Place

You don't absolutely have to finish that report after dinner. Your spouse has been waiting all day to see you and spend time with you. Now's your chance to get some fresh air, spend some quality time with your honey. That report can wait until you're fresh in the morning. You have to be careful that your work doesn't spill into family time. Just because you work from home doesn't mean you should be available all hours of the day. There is a danger of putting in too many hours or overworking. As improbable as this might sound, imagine that it's 11 p.m. and you suddenly have a panic attack about work. It's all too easy to go into your home office and work until 1 a.m. Be sure you switch your focus to family. Keep work and family separate.

Being at home ALL THE TIME.

You might need to take a day off every couple of weeks and get out into the world to see that yes, other people still do exist! Keep up those social skills, talk with people in the grocery store or elevator. Always carry your business cards though, just in case.

Money

Retirement - Working online - especially freelancing - does not usually have bonuses, health benefits or insurance. There are flush times and lean times when you are running your own home business. You are even more responsible to save money for those dry spells and save a portion for your retirement.

Math

Bookkeeping may be new to you for running your own work from home business.   Open another bank account for all your work money. You'll need to keep business and personal funds separate. Make a spreadsheet for all the money you receive and the invoice number. Keep all receipts. In a file. In order. Keep track of your income. It's a good idea to issue numbered invoices to clients. Keep a copy of each invoice. Keep a file for everything that you'll need for your tax return. Tax is complicated, it may be worth seeking the advice of a professional qualified accountant. They can save you money, worry and stress. There are tons of bookkeeping programs out there, research them and pick the one that suits you and your business the best. Checkout Invoiceable, Curdbee, Freshbooks, some are free, some are fee based. Take your pick!

Now that you are focused and working with a strong goal in mind, you need to stay healthy.

Chapter 7 - Staying Healthy

Doctors are seeing more business owners who work from a home office with a number of common health concerns.

Isolation

Working from a home office can be lonely. We miss out on coffee breaks with colleagues. Schedule networking as part of your business. This will help with loneliness, but also will help your business as you make connections.

Get out of the house regularly, even to have a coffee on the deck. See what the weather is like outside! Take the dog for a walk around the neighbourhood before you start your day or as a break from sitting midday.

Sleep

Take advantage of the fact that you are working from home and don't have to get up early. No more hour long commutes! Take that time and translate it into a full night's sleep. Wake up refreshed and your energy level will be stabilized throughout the day.

Control Your Destiny

You will be in an ideal office environment —you're in charge. Open the windows and let in some fresh air to reinvigorate yourself, set the thermostat to whatever temperature feels most comfortable and turn on or off as many lights as you need to see without squinting or dealing with glare.

Issues with Eating

When working at home, many of us tend to concentrate and plow through the work, not taking time to eat. When we finally take a break we over-eat as blood sugar levels have dropped and we are starving! Have nutritious snacks on hand including some protein and good fat in each snack. For example – a handful of pumpkin seeds with 3 dried apricots, or a sliced apple with 1 tbsp of almond butter or other nut butter

On the other hand working at home can also mean over-eating as the refrigerator is always nearby. Shovelling food in your mouth while reading all those emails is a bad habit.

Get your family in on the action. After your scheduled work day is over, spend some quality time with the family outside playing games like badminton, throwing a ball around or back yard soccer.

Keep active, its good for the mind, body and soul.

Neck, shoulder/wrist strain injuries and low back pain

These health issues generally relate to work station set up in the home office.

Here's a checklist for the ergonomics of any office.

Keyboard Position

Upper arms hang relaxed at side during computer use

Elbow joints are at about 90 degrees

Hands are in line with forearms when using keyboard and/or mouse

Monitor Position

The top of the screen is at eye height

Viewing distance is 18 - 24 inches

Monitor is centered in front of user

Seating

Thighs are roughly parallel to the floor

Feet are flat on the floor or on a footrest.

Lighting

Computer screen is free of glare spots

Eyes are shielded from sources of direct glare

Office area is illuminated with indirect light fixtures

Desk should have adjustable task light

Working from a home office means missing out on that 10 minute walk to the bus or from the car to the office, and we don't take breaks with colleagues. Sitting too long at even a properly set up work area can lead to postural problems. Schedule breaks to get up from your desk. Try setting tiny goals –"get 3 phone calls or 3 emails done ... then I can go have a break on the deck."

Now you are healthy, focused and ready to work. What time to start work, how long, when to take breaks?   Let's set up a schedule.

Chapter 8 - Setting a Schedule

You need a solid schedule to keep yourself from getting derailed while working at home.

It might be beneficial for some, while others might find it difficult to cope with. However, following certain measures and sticking to it would prove working from home to be a boon.

It's better to have a separate work area for all the home business activities so you can focus on business during work hours. By enabling separate access to clients and family members, there cannot be any interference between the two. A fixed schedule is beneficial for anyone planning to set up a home business. This way, there will be a cap on the times that clients would be visiting and the rest of the time can be devoted to the family.

Try to fix work time based on your spouse's work hours and children's school hours. Having a schedule such that you get to spend a fair amount of time with your loved ones will generate a positive vibe so that you can get comfortable while working too. Plan social gatherings well in advance so that you make time for them by varying your schedules accordingly.

There should be a pre-calculated number of non-working days. The non-working days that are decided can be used for family outings or spend quality time with family. Ultimately, satisfying the needs of your family and being with them whenever they need you would satisfy everyone. Comply strictly with the working hours you have decided on and channel all your attention towards your business in the stipulated working hours and on the same lines, during your family time too.

It is a herculean task to strike a balance between a home business and your family. Prioritize and list down your needs regarding the family and business. This way, you can get a clear picture about what should be chosen over what and work accordingly in any situation. There will never be a dilemma or conflict in your mind about what to do next or what to choose.

A successful home business and a contented family life rarely co-exist. Optimum management needs to exist so that both ends are managed and you can be prosperous without making your family life suffer. Everyone in the family needs to know the schedule you've set.

Work when you say you will, and don't work when you say you will not.
When spouse and kids know they will get your full attention later, it makes waiting easier.

You are now in a nice workspace, working away with family waiting for the end of your workday. You are well fed and

focused. Business slow? Want to play outside instead?   How
will you stay motivated?

Chapter 9 - How to Stay Motivated and Productive

There's something almost rhythmical about the 9-5 grind. The alarm clock sounds at 7am. You get out of bed. You eat. You shower. Then you begin your commute into work. Upon arrival, you find everything has been laid out for you. Your schedule, your quarterly targets, even your list of break times - have all been pre-determined before you got in. All that's left for you to do is just sit back and flow with everything.

Productivity in the workplace stops being an action and becomes a habit. Your boss makes sure motivation levels never drop, by wielding the possibility of unemployment high above your head, like an axe. The whole process of going to work, reaching your goals and maintaining productivity, begins to work on autopilot. Then... one day...for whatever reason, you leave... And it stops.

On the surface of things, working from home sounds like the dream job. Wake up whenever you want to, shower around noon, spend the whole day drinking coffee, checking emails and snacking on delicious cookies.

Then at the end of it, collect a cool looking paycheck for your troubles. Many people do live like this - and they have lots of fun doing so. But for some, working at home can lead to stagnation. Unless they self-motivate. When starting a home business - everything you've ever learned about motivation in your life changes, overnight. All of a sudden there's no parent, teacher or boss to keep you going anymore... There's only you. When the initial excitement of working for yourself wears off, you're faced with a new challenge - to keep it all going.

Strategies to improve motivation and productivity have had more books written about them than libraries across the world can hold. Motivation is big business. It's very often the difference between success at something or failure. Working from home is no different. A topic for maintaining motivation that many books like to talk about... is routine. Human beings are creatures of habit. One of the greatest ways to stay motivated and remain productive in the work at home world, is to keep a routine. Even when it feels like you don't need to. No boss around doesn't mean that life should become a free-for-all. It's tempting to go to bed whenever you want and wake up whenever the mood strikes, but ask yourself: Is this really going to be a habit that brings the best out of me? It's unlikely. Studies show that maintaining a proper sleep pattern is crucial for brain function and that poor sleeping habits can reduce productivity by up to 25%! A regular sleep pattern is like the stitch that holds your life together in the correct balance. Don't neglect it.

A great way to increase motivation and productivity is to hack into your subconscious mind in order to get the most out of yourself. Your subconscious is the greatest strategist the world has ever known, so use it to your advantage.

Many home business owners communicate to their subconscious that what they're doing isn't very important... even though it most certainly is! Working from home doesn't mean that you should lounge around all day in those grey pajamas with a tear in the side of them. Unless you have darn good productivity in those unsexy grey eyesores get out of them already!

Think of the message that sends out to your subconscious. Nothing says 'lower productivity please" quite like being in your pajamas at 1 in the afternoon. Dress presentably. Be ready for anything. There's no need to put on a suit to work at home, but by putting on some actual clothes and fixing your hair, you'll prompt your brain to take the day more seriously. Productivity levels will thank you for it in the long run. By all means dress casually and comfortably. You are at home after all. This is where the whole term "Open Collar" began. Relax!

The biggest temptation 'work at home' folk face is staying put in our little offices all day. When your income is in the palm of hands and you can make more money simply by fulfilling another order, why would you ever want to leave the house?! Well, because there's a world out there. The motivation for doing what we're doing was to gain more freedom and greater independence. Why then, do we seem to end up with less? We lose balance.

We lose balance by letting our lives become lopsided. And that's a disaster. With a little practice we become great at implementing a strategy in order to gain more traffic to our sites or improve our conversion rates. Unfortunately though, we become bad at developing a strategy just to do the simplest of things, like step outside for a while, socializing and exercising. If you want better productivity and more motivation: Turn off your laptop for an hour a day and go outside. Sit on a bench somewhere and eat lunch.

Make it a part of your business strategy to incorporate relaxing times into your day. It will keep you fresh for years to come. If you must work, try to take your laptop to a coffee shop, or do a little work in the garden (wifi permitting.)

Talk to anybody that runs a work at home business and you'll hear the same thing: It becomes an obsession. It's one of the finest things you can feel, generating a sale for the first time. You've done it. Nobody else. Just you. It sets in motion one of the most rewarding and satisfying hobbies or careers that's possible to have... Making money for yourself.

But now you're in danger of burnout. Many people go tooth and nail after their first victory, trying to work every hour under the sun to make more money or have more success. If you're not careful, too much of a good thing can bad for you. There's a fine line between enthusiasm and unhealthy obsession. Don't let what could be a profitable hobby or career for you, tire you out or become a chore.

Take part in different activities. Keep your mind fresh. Burnout is a thunderstorm that rains down on the fires of motivation and productivity, putting out the inferno. Have something else in your life that you enjoy doing, other than making money.

Treat your other hobbies in a Zen like fashion. When you're doing them, concentrate on them. Don't allow your mind to keep wandering back to your online ventures. Motivation and productivity are far too valuable a thing to have extinguished.

The internet offers more ways to distract yourself than an Xbox inside a candy store full of supermodels. Whether you're a fan of addictive strategy games, or just love reading newspapers online - there's nothing quite like the internet for taking your focus away from work. You may be pretty darn motivated when it comes to raising your World Of Warcraft rankings. Here's one of the best tips for keeping a constant level of productivity, when running a home business. LOG THE HECK OUT OF TWITTER AND CLOSE FACEBOOK ALREADY!!!! (As long as they aren't for business purposes.) Both will suck the productivity out of you like a vampire feeding on the sweetness of your results. Have you ever heard somebody say "Spending the day on Facebook really helped me get a lot done today..." Didn't think so.

Have a time for work and a time for play. Regular breaks are a good thing. Using Facebook chat when trying to analyze conversion data? Not so much. Mixing business and pleasure is never, ever, ever a good idea!

I think you are ready.

Chapter 10 - Conclusion

Just by buying this book, you have proven you have a wealth of characteristics you should be proud of. You have bravery - venturing into this "work at home" industry. You have problem solving skills - you wouldn't have made a cent otherwise. You have self-motivation. You are out here working for yourself, going it alone. You're already a winner.

Whether you're making the amount of money you want to or not, this final step for staying motivated and productive is all about fun. Ladies and gentleman... REWARD YOURSELF. We're all in this business to make money and to be more independent. It's important never to forget that.

To make money on the intergalactic web means you have done a large amount of research, self study, practice and reading. And that's impressive. You deserve rewarding for what you do. You also deserve recognition. There comes a time when every work at home entrepreneur must look at themselves in the mirror and say 'Great job sport.'

There also comes a time when you're due a bonus. A productive work week deserves a bottle of wine and a pizza takeaway on Fridays. Increasing your sales figures means you deserve a shopping trip. Perhaps record profit this month means you deserve a holiday away from the computer. It will all come down to you. Life can't be all stick and no carrot. You'll get so much more out of yourself when you enjoy what you're working towards.

Even if your motivation levels are fine and productivity good, at least this book has shown you a blueprint of what not to do when working at home. The important thing to remember when working at home, is to actually work. Though sometimes it's equally as important not to work. You'll find a balance that suits you. If you mull over just a couple of points mentioned here, productivity and motivation will be fine for you.

Here's a quick checklist of "things to do":

- o Make a list of the way you personally will save money by working at home. Put down close estimations of actual dollar amounts
- o Research online opportunities carefully. Check out Snopes for scams
- o Think long and hard about what you are passionate about. Do you want to use your hobby to make money or keep it as a hobby for fun?
- o Pick the spot in your home for your office.

- o Make your new workspace work for you. Make it bright, clean and "you".
- o Commit to working at home and don't get distracted.
- o Be Healthy. Eat, sleep and make money.
- o Stay motivated. Remember why you are in that new office.

Congratulations on taking this first step. Hope this home job offers you better opportunities for growth and helps you in achieving your dreams.

About the author

Kimberley Suter left an office job to raise a family for 10 years. Once the time was right, Kim began a new career working from home. She learned the ins and outs of the successful home office and balancing life, children, husband and home for herself through trial and error and experimentation.

Author's Disclaimer

This book is designed to provide information and motivation to our readers. It is sold with the understanding that the publisher is not engaged to render any type of psychological, legal, or any other kind of professional advice. The content of each article is the sole expression and opinion of its author, and not necessarily that of the publisher. No warranties or guarantees are expressed or implied by the publisher's choice to include any of the content in this volume. Neither the publisher nor the individual author(s) shall be liable for any physical, psychological, emotional, financial, or commercial damages, including, but not limited to, special, incidental, consequential or other damages. Our views and rights are the same: You are responsible for your own choices, actions, and results.